AF006421

Lynnea Hagen on Stuckness

140 Insights and Tips to Get Unstuck, Get Going, and Get What You Want

By Lynnea Hagen

An Actionable Success Journal

E-mail: info@thinkaha.com
20660 Stevens Creek Blvd., Suite 210
Cupertino, CA 95014

Copyright © 2015, Lynnea Hagen

All rights reserved. No part of this book shall be reproduced, stored in a retrieval system, or transmitted by any means electronic, mechanical, photocopying, recording, or otherwise without written permission from the publisher.

> ⇨ Please pick up a copy of this book in the Aha Amplifier and share each AhaMessage socially at http://aha.pub/stuckness

Published by THiNKaha®
20660 Stevens Creek Blvd., Suite 210, Cupertino, CA 95014
http://thinkaha.com
E-mail: info@thinkaha.com

First Printing: October 2015
Paperback ISBN: 978-1-61699-162-3 (1-61699-162-3)
eBook ISBN: 978-1-61699-145-6 (1-61699-145-3)
Place of Publication: Silicon Valley, California, USA
Paperback Library of Congress Number: 2015950352

Trademarks

All terms mentioned in this book that are known to be trademarks or service marks have been appropriately capitalized. Neither THiNKaha, nor any of its imprints, can attest to the accuracy of this information. Use of a term in this book should not be regarded as affecting the validity of any trademark or service mark.

Warning and Disclaimer

Every effort has been made to make this book as complete and as accurate as possible. The information provided is on an "as is" basis. The author(s), publisher, and their agents assume no responsibility for errors or omissions. Nor do they assume liability or responsibility to any person or entity with respect to any loss or damages arising from the use of information contained herein.

Reviews for Lynnea Hagen on Stuckness Book

"Lynnea Hagen is a masterful coach who has shed light on what all of us feel at one time or another: stuck! In Lynnea Hagen on Stuckness, she provides an easy-to-digest manuscript with a journaling component that is simple to follow. Written in short bites, the book is a great way to jumpstart any activity you're feeling stuck on. A terrific read that gives a little push to help you get going. I highly recommend this book."

Erika Taylor Montgomery, CEO-Chief Publicist, Three Girls Media, Inc.

"This collection will certainly be looked at differently by different people, depending on their perspective. I found it practical and true to life. Some tips hit you right in the eye; some are even funny. Thank you, Lynnea, for sharing and bringing this delightful reminder to our daily existence, to help us find more meaning and solutions to get unstuck in career and in life."

Anolia Facun, Best-selling Author, Founder of What a Wonderful World Enterprise

"Warning: I do NOT recommend Lynnea Hagen on Stuckness to anyone who is content with life "as-is," is willing to settle for mediocrity, or who thinks it's "good enough" to stay where they are. However, if you want a "fire to be lit under your butt," there isn't a more memorable, concise, and catchy way to get yourself up and moving than by reading every empowering quote in this book, journaling on it, and sharing it with your friends!

My favorite tip was #43: "Get Unstuck: Hang with people who are your 'firelighters,' and walk away from the 'fire extinguishers.' @LynneaHagen" (and there are countless other great quotes where that came from!)

Thank you, Lynnea Hagen – The "Get Unstuck" Queen – for re-kindling a fire in me! And now that it's lit, there's no way I'm letting myself – or anyone else – put it out!

And I am committed to spreading this fire to women entrepreneurs everywhere, especially those who want to make more progress this year than they have in the past five years – and sustain it!"

Josephine "Jos" Hanan, CEO/Founder of Promote HER Business

"No one is immune from "stuckness" in space and time. If you discover that you are stuck at any time, you can get unstuck by following Lynnea Hagen's tips and insights in her new book, Lynnea Hagen on Stuckness. *By focusing on 140 tips, each one no more than 140 characters, Lynnea's book rapidly facilitates unstuckness. If you or team members are currently trapped in a dungeon of stuckness, get Lynnea's book to become unstuck. If you are not, get Lynnea's book for someone you know who may be stuck. Lynnea Hagen's* Lynnea Hagen on Stuckness *may be the best book you could give friends, relatives, and colleagues who would like to rapidly sail from a "red sea of stuckness" to a "blue ocean of boundless opportunities"."*

Rod King, PhD, Business Coach on Ambidextrous Leadership & Growth Strategy President of Red Ocean Disruption (ROD) University

How to Read a THiNKaha® Book
A Note from the Publisher

The THiNKaha series is the CliffsNotes of the 21st century. The value of these books is that they are contextual in nature. Although the actual words won't change, their meaning will change every time you read one as your context will change. Experience your own "aha!" moments ("AhaMessages™") with a THiNKaha book; AhaMessages are looked at as "actionable" moments—think of a specific project you're working on, an event, a sales deal, a personal issue, etc. and see how the AhaMessages in this book can inspire your own AhaMessages, something that you can specifically act on. Here's how to read one of these books and have it work for you.

1. Read a THiNKaha book (these slim and handy books should only take about 15-20 minutes of your time!) and write down one to three actionable items you thought of while reading it. Each journal-style THiNKaha book is equipped with space for you to write down your notes and thoughts underneath each AhaMessage.

2. Mark your calendar to re-read this book again in 30 days.

3. Repeat step #1 and write down one to three more AhaMessages that grab you this time. I guarantee that they will be different than the first time. BTW: this is also a great time to reflect on the actions taken from the last set of AhaMessages you wrote down.

After reading a THiNKaha book, writing down your AhaMessages, re-reading it, and writing down more AhaMessages, you'll begin to see how these books contextually apply to you. THiNKaha books advocate for continuous, lifelong learning. They will help you transform your ahas into actionable items with tangible results until you no longer have to say "aha!" to these moments—they'll become part of your daily practice as you continue to grow and learn.

As Chief Aha Instigator & CEO of THiNKaha, I definitely practice what I preach. I read *Alexisms* and *Ted Rubin on How to Look People in the Eye Digitally*, and one new book once a month and take away two to three different action items from each of them every time. Please e-mail me your ahas today!

Mitchell Levy
publisher@thinkaha.com

Dedication

My grandparents came from the "old country" in the early 20th century, armed only with an 8th grade education and a huge amount of grit. They raised 11 wonderful children, including my mother, on a coal miner's income and a ton of love. My father was raised on a small Iowa farm, and though he never received a high school diploma, became an Air Force pilot and successful business owner. The spunk, spirit, wisdom, and integrity of these people continue to inspire me to keep going and growing. My twin sons, Aaron and Joshua, taught me, a single mom, to be strong and courageous, set loving boundaries, take care of myself, and communicate cleanly. All these people gave me great gifts. In gratitude and love, I dedicate this book to them.

Acknowledgments

I want to thank Bill Leonard, my accountability buddy as we each committed to finish our prospective books. Thank you, Mitchell Levy of Happy About, who created (and introduced me to) the THiNKaha® book process. Mitchell, it's brilliant! Finally, I want to thank the CEO and founder of Promote HER Business, Josephine Hanan, for being an amazing encourager and cheerleader.

Contents

Foreword — 11

Section I
What Is "Stuckness" — 15

Section II
What Causes "Stuckness" — 21

Section III
How to Get Unstuck — 33

Section IV
Get Going and Stay Unstuck — 109

About the Author — 117

Foreword

I have been a speaker, trainer, coach, manager, and consultant for over 35 years (I'm shocked, too. Yes, I started when I was seven). I have worked in, for, or in service to family-owned businesses, small businesses, huge corporations, and non-profits of all shapes, sorts, and stripes. Personally, I have a tendency to want to try new things, jump in and learn to swim later, or "do it all," all at once. I have also experienced extreme personal losses and challenges. It's because of all the above that I have, I have become an expert in "stuckness" (my word) in myself, others, and organizations.

"Stuckness" hurts. It can hurt on many levels. It can dig into our self-esteem, relationships, and income. In a business, stuckness can undermine decisions, teamwork, projects, and progress. It can drain the potential to thrive, not only for the organization, but also for its people. That's not okay to me. The intention of this book is to provide relief from the pain by providing simple wisdom, insights, steps, and "kick in the butt" tidbits.

I like simple. But the truth is, we're complex critters in an increasingly complex world. I think Henry David Thoreau had it right when he said, "Simplify, simplify, simplify." Easy to say when you're living and reflecting at Walden Pond in 1854, not so much today. So how do we, as 21st century beings, simplify so that we can more easily breathe and be who and what we need to be? To achieve with clarity what we need to achieve?

As a speaker, I've been asked to simplify getting unstuck by answering this question: What is the ONE thing I'd recommend doing in order to get unstuck? Here's my "bad news, good news" answer: There is no one thing. There are two things. They are simple, but not simplistic. They can be used to positively impact teams as well as entire organizations.

First, be inspired by inspiring yourself. What is it about YOU that inspires you? For me, it's my ability to see possibilities. From there, move to find the great inner core, or what I call your "Golden Purpose" (GP) of why you are on Planet Earth. Then let that work for you from the inside out: to let trivialities slip away, to delegate, to honor yourself and others, to have healthy boundaries and clearer plans and strategies, to shed what (and who) drains you, and to stop wasting your precious time. My Golden Purpose is to create a more loving and sustainable planet. It's simple, it's big, and it inspires me. It makes me say, "WOW!" As I became clear on my GP, the "hows" emerged naturally, and my own stuckness dissipated. What is the Golden Purpose for you or your organization? (Contact me for more information and support on this vital step – a process I call "the profitability of Purpose," for it can can elevate revenues, profits, and productivity for individuals and entire companies).

Second, fill your mind with gratitude: in the morning, list five things you are grateful for, and list five more before you go to sleep at night. It will quiet your head and soul and open your mind to positive possibilities. We're all grateful for "big things" – family, health, our house. That's easy stuff. I challenge you to go into the little corners and moments of your life and of your day, and be grateful for the person who let you into traffic, or fixed your technology problem, or grew your veggies. If you can sit up and feed yourself or pet your dog, those are pretty incredible things to be grateful for. Do this "gratitude challenge," and truly, your life will change . . . and you will start to experience less "stuckness."

By doing these two simple things – defining your Golden Purpose and being fully grateful – you should find it easy to incorporate the insights and tips in this simple little book, and experience a more successful, abundant business AND life.

Bloom big.

Lynnea Hagen, October 2015

Section I
What Is "Stuckness"

The truth is, "stuckness", i.e., the state of being or feeling stuck or off-track, is part of the human condition. In this state, you may feel unable to move on a project, relationship, decision, or creative endeavor. Your mind may feel closed down; paths may not seem apparent. You may spend much of your time doing "busy work" and avoiding important tasks. You may feel blocked off from yourself. You've heard of "writer's block," right? That is a form of stuckness. Even great composers go through a seasons of stuckness. Rachmaninoff experienced a huge period of stuckness and believed that his composing days were over. He used the services of a hypnotherapist and was finally able to break out of his stuckness and compose fantastic pieces that are still enjoyed today. So when you are experiencing stuckness, be assured that you are in good company (you just don't want to stay there!)

Section I: What Is "Stuckness"

1

We're ALL stuck from time to time, AND we all deserve to live fully, to be, have & do fulfilling things with our precious lives. @LynneaHagen

_____

_____

_____

2

Stuckness feels like one foot is nailed to the floor - you're moving, but only in a circle and not going anywhere. @LynneaHagen

_____

_____

_____

3

Stuckness is like having rocks in your pocket, while trying to fly. You flap your wings & try to soar, but can't rise up. @LynneaHagen.

_____

_____

_____

Section I: What Is "Stuckness"

4

Stuckness closes down efforts & "possibility thinking" when things don't look as you'd like, and you can't seem to get past it. @LynneaHagen

_____

_____

_____

5

Stuckness may show up as low productivity, which leaves us feeling "less than," and is often self-perpetuating. @LynneaHagen

_____

_____

_____

6

Stuckness: You can't get started on a task, or change a situation. Often characterized by procrastination and low focus.
@LynneaHagen

_____

_____

_____

7

Stuckness is when you feel overwhelmed, bogged down, stalled - without decisions, clear steps ahead, or movement.
@LynneaHagen

_____

_____

_____

Section II
What Causes "Stuckness"

As mentioned in the foreword, we are complex beings, living in a complex and demanding world. We are often trying to please several people or projects at once, without taking time to do quality thinking. We live in noisy, reactive places, mentally *and* physically, and our focus suffers as a result. We often don't take time to do quality planning or create boundaries around our time and energy. I often see this in business owners and leaders, who pride themselves in "open door policies" or waste their time in micromanaging others (then wonder why they themselves can't seem to accomplish anything). We also may not ask for what we need, and we become exhausted. Stuckness can be a complex situation.

Section II: What Causes "Stuckness"

8

Stuckness is caused by our energies being drained by too many interferences, obligations & little things pulling us off path. @LynneaHagen

_____

_____

_____

9

Stuckness is caused by giving attention to too many little things, at the expense of our physical, emotional & spiritual self. @LynneaHagen

_____

_____

_____

10

Stuckness is caused by trying to do it all, not delegating, not setting priorities, not guarding our precious time. @LynneaHagen

---

11

Stuckness is caused by putting others' needs before our own via "open door policies," and allowing non-urgent interruptions. @LynneaHagen

Section II: What Causes "Stuckness"

12

Stuckness is caused by beliefs & thoughts that we're never going to be good enough, or that things have to be done perfectly. @LynneaHagen

_____

_____

_____

13

Stuckness can be caused by not knowing what you really want, or what type of person you're committed to being. @LynneaHagen

14

Stuckness is caused by focusing on what's wrong by trying to correct errors, or focusing on what may go wrong. @LynneaHagen

Section II: What Causes "Stuckness"

15

Stuckness is caused by a worldview based on scarcity, not abundance or surplus. Or by having too low standards with ourselves.
@LynneaHagen

_____

_____

_____

16

Stuckness is caused by allowing fear to control our actions and decisions, especially fear that we'll mess up. @LynneaHagen

_____

_____

_____

17

Stuckness is caused by subtle belief: "Today will be like yesterday," focusing on the past & believing it defines your future. @LynneaHagen

_____

_____

_____

Section II: What Causes "Stuckness"

18

Stuckness is cause & effect. It is caused by our thinking, ideas, feeling, beliefs & expectations. @LynneaHagen

_____
_____
_____

19

Stuckness is cause & effect. The effects are things - relationships, actions, results, movement - that our thinking causes. @LynneaHagen

20

Stuckness caused by forgetting our dreams. Most of us give up on our dreams or compromise them to what we think is realistic. @marciawieder

Section II: What Causes "Stuckness"

21

Stuckness is caused by focusing on obstacles and taking focus off positive possibilities, goals, or dreams.
@LynneaHagen

_____

_____

_____

22

Stuckness is caused by ignoring this: We bring all of who we are into everything. Personal You & Business You are intertwined. @LynneaHagen

23

Stuckness can be caused by our having too few boundaries, or too little integrity with ourselves & others. @LynneaHagen

Section III
How to Get Unstuck

In this section, I offer numerous tips on getting out of the state of "stuckness." There is no "one size fits all" approach. As complex beings in a complex world, we may require time and patience to get "unstuck" and be fully on our way. Just know that it is time well-invested in yourself and what you are here to accomplish personally and professionally. Use the space provided to make notes, cite personal examples, create your own "to do" list, or project plan for your path forward.

Here are a couple of bonus tips for this section. Feel free to share them with your friends, followers, or team:

When you start dwelling on the past, be grateful for the experience & everyone in it & how you have learned and grown. @LynneaHagen

Remember, it's always too soon to give up. Never give up; the next moment may be holding a miracle. Affirm this every day. @LynneaHagen

Section III: How to Get Unstuck

24

Get Unstuck. Stop focusing on obstacles. Focus on goals. Realize that obstacles can't be removed by putting attention on them. @LynneaHagen

_____
_____
_____

25

Get unstuck. Don't let someone else's time wasters be your time wasters; e.g., emails, Facebook, complaining, gossiping, etc. @LynneaHagen

_____

_____

_____

Section III: How to Get Unstuck

26

Get unstuck. Get a fresh set of eyes to look at what you're doing & how. Get a coach, friend, colleague to see your situation. @LynneaHagen

_____

_____

_____

27

Get unstuck: Get organized! It takes time, BUT gives time, energy & results; could ease your overwhelm & be the fuel you need.
@LynneaHagen

Section III: How to Get Unstuck

28

Get unstuck: Release resentment and blame. Define your purpose and passion, and your focus and energy will improve. @LynneaHagen

_____

_____

_____

29

Get unstuck: Take a weekend, or a whole week if necessary, to explore who you are now and who you want to be. @marciawieder

_____

_____

_____

30

Get unstuck. Ask questions like, "What is it I love? How do I want my life to be? What am I willing to do about that?" @marciawieder

_____

_____

_____

31

Get unstuck. Adopt a "promotion focus." Do something because you see it as a way to end up better off than you are now. @HGHalvorson

_____

_____

_____

Section III: How to Get Unstuck

32

Get Unstuck. Use your anxiety & doubt. Adopt "prevention focus." See the task as a way to keep what you've got, to avoid loss. @HGHalvorson

_____
_____
_____

33

Get Unstuck: Don't focus on what you don't have! Shift to a view of Universal surplus, abundance. Be grateful for small things! @LynneaHagen

---

34

Get Unstuck. Ask: What do I want, and why don't I have it? What would I like to be doing, and why aren't I? @RLRlearning

Section III: How to Get Unstuck

35

Get Unstuck. Ask: What do I want to eliminate to clear the path forward, and why haven't I done that? @RLRlearning

_____

_____

_____

36

Get unstuck. Focus: Shut yourself away from distractions. Turn off all phones. Set a timer for 60-90 minutes. Do the task.
@LynneaHagen

_____
_____
_____

Section III: How to Get Unstuck

37

Get unstuck. Approach the day with the curiosity of a 3-year-old. If it's not quite right yet, be curious. Keep asking "Why?" @LynneaHagen

38

Get unstuck. Create a big, audacious, exciting, mouth-watering, make-you-cry plan, adventure, or vision for one year from now. @LynneaHagen

39

Get unstuck. Keep your big, audacious, exciting, mouth-watering, make-you-cry plan, adventure, or vision in front of you. @LynneaHagen

_____
_____
_____

Section III: How to Get Unstuck

40

Get unstuck. Notice your Inner Critic. Notice its message to you & know that you do NOT need to heed its warnings. @wingsforwomen

_____

_____

_____

41

Get unstuck. If it's hard, boring, unpleasant, use if-then planning: "If X happens, then I'll do Y." Set a what, when & where. @HGHalvorson

_____

_____

_____

42

Assume it's possible for you to have what you want. Raise possibilities. Probability WON'T help you move. Possibility will. @RLRlearning

43

Get Unstuck: Hang with people who are your "fire lighters," and walk away from the "fire extinguishers." @LynneaHagen

Section III: How to Get Unstuck

44

Get unstuck. Turn "you" into a science experiment. Ask "What do I want that'd prove my success professionally & personally?" @RLRlearning

_____

_____

_____

45

Get unstuck. Envision & "language" yourself into the next phase. Focus on future dates, time, assignment based on today's action. @artdcoach

46

Get unstuck. Take imperfect action. Movement causes momentum. Moving in the wrong direction is better than no movement at all. @LynneaHagen

Section III: How to Get Unstuck

47

Get unstuck. Realize you can't make a mistake, you can only make a decision for your next best step; you have nothing to lose! @LynneaHagen

_____

_____

_____

48

Get unstuck. Find someone to inspire you to do better than you may know or believe with your limited knowledge/experience. @LynneaHagen

_____

_____

_____

Section III: How to Get Unstuck

49

Get unstuck. Be like Spock & ignore your feelings. In order to do something, you don't need to "feel" like doing it. @HGHalvorson

50

Get Unstuck. Stop comparing yourself to others. Don't compare your "inside" to their "outside." Focus on your own path. @LynneaHagen

51

Get unstuck. Realize that the past brings you to the present. Use it as fuel, not as a rearview mirror. @LynneaHagen

_____
_____
_____

Section III: How to Get Unstuck

52

Get unstuck. Be careful on what you feed your mind, body & spirit. It's all tied together & will either "feed or bleed you."
@LynneaHagen

53

Get Unstuck. Consider what you do for "Version One," which takes pressure off having to create "perfection."
@LynneaHagen

54

Get Unstuck: Find someone who's worse off than you are & help them. It puts life in perspective, and will lift you up. @LynneaHagen.

55

Get unstuck. Carry a goal card with something you're working to achieve. Look at it often each day. @LynneaHagen

Section III: How to Get Unstuck

56

Get Unstuck. Create a support system of others with goals. Set a day & time to connect, discuss challenges, share achievements. @LynneaHagen

57

Get Unstuck. Believe in the possibility of reconnecting with your passion and what makes you tick. @marciawieder

58

Get unstuck: When you feel tension, STOP. Do nothing for a few minutes. Breathe, relax, open your mind to possibilities. @LynneaHagen

59

Get unstuck. MOVE! Every 2 hours go for a fast walk. This brings oxygen & clarity to your brain, with new energy & perspective. @LynneaHagen

_____
_____
_____

60

To get unstuck: LOOK! What's around you, what can you use, how far have you come, what got you here? @LynneaHagen

Section III: How to Get Unstuck

61

To get unstuck: LOOK! What helped others before you? What have you missed? There's a path there! @LynneaHagen

62

Get unstuck: LISTEN! To your still, small inner "voice" of love, guidance, wisdom, insight, and encouragement. @LynneaHagen

63

Get unstuck: LISTEN! To the voices of love, guidance, wisdom, insight, and encouragement of others around you.
@LynneaHagen

Section III: How to Get Unstuck

64

Get unstuck. UNPLUG from time wasters, busy-ness, noise, draining relationships, interruptions & too many commitments. @LynneaHagen

_____
_____
_____

65

Get unstuck. Change your words. Redefine your work from what you HAVE to do, to what you GET to do! @LynneaHagen

_____
_____
_____

66

Get unstuck. Clean up, release, minimize what keeps you awake at night. Create reserves: money, support, friends, health, love. @LynneaHagen

67

Get unstuck. Read, watch, listen, surround yourself with positive things. Positivity will raise your energy and focus. @LynneaHagen

Section III: How to Get Unstuck

68

Get unstuck. Put your time, mind, energy into positive environments. Your mind will think most about what it's most exposed to. @LynneaHagen

69

Get unstuck. Get rid of saboteurs: anger, resentment, bitterness, self-hatred, anxiety with daily 5 minutes of gratitude.
@Lynnea Hagen

70

Get unstuck. Get rid of inner saboteurs, especially unforgiveness, Make amends, forgive, ask for forgiveness, forgive yourself.
@LynneaHagen

71

Get Unstuck. Be clean in all areas: communications with others, your surroundings, your beliefs about yourself. @LynneaHagen

_____

_____

_____

72

Get Unstuck. Be healthy in all areas: relationships, your body, your self-talk, your environments, how others treat you.
@LynneaHagen

Section III: How to Get Unstuck

73

Get unstuck. Absorb this thinking: You cannot make a mistake, you can only make a decision that will be your next best step. @LynneaHagen

_____

_____

_____

74

Get unstuck. Know that you can't wait for a perfect time or perfect conditions. "Wherever you are is the entry point." - Kabir. @LynneaHagen

_____

_____

_____

75

Get unstuck. Face the truth about your abilities for willpower or your capacity for self-control & ability to "power through."
@LynneaHagen

_____

_____

_____

Section III: How to Get Unstuck

76

Get unstuck. In all you are and do: make sure you are getting your mental, emotional, physical needs met. @LynneaHagen

77

Get Unstuck. Get an accountability partner or coach to help keep you true to what you say you want, or are going to do. @LynneaHagen

78

Get unstuck. Stop obsessing over "getting even" or "getting my share." Stop acting & thinking like a victim. Stay your path. @LynneaHagen

79

Compartmentalize areas of focus into mental "rooms." Open this "room," focus, then close the compartment. Move on to next area. @RyanBlair

Section III: How to Get Unstuck

80

Get unstuck. Resolve to only look forward, to the future. Remember that the past does NOT equal the future. @LynneaHagen

_____

_____

_____

81

Get unstuck. Use your body's natural rhythm: work for 90 minutes, renew for 10. Repeat. Focus and productivity will increase.
@LynneaHagen

82

Get Unstuck. Create a support system of others with goals. Remind each other of your goals, dreams, infinite potential.
@bobproctorLIVE

Section III: How to Get Unstuck

83

Get unstuck. Get a handle on chaos by PLANNING! 1 minute of planning saves 9 minutes of chaos, 30 minutes saves 4.5 hours. @LynneaHagen

_____

_____

_____

84

Clean up what you're tolerating: stress, your thoughts, self-talk, feelings, relationships, interruptions, reactions. @LynneaHagen

Section III: How to Get Unstuck

85

Clean up what you're tolerating: broken things in your home, office, car; how others treat you; how you treat yourself. @LynneaHagen

_____

_____

_____

86

Get unstuck. Stop telling yourself that you're stuck, stressed, or overwhelmed, which creates more of the same. @LynneaHagen

_____

_____

_____

87

Get Unstuck. Eliminate little irritations. They rob your focus, and create mental "regrouping time" and more internal friction. @LynneaHagen

Section III: How to Get Unstuck

88

Get unstuck. Get 7-8 hours of sleep - this will improve your focus, outlook, and ability to sit and work. @LynneaHagen

89

Get unstuck. Stop eating bad fats and sugars, which slow your body, brain functions, and your ability to think and focus. @LynneaHagen

90

Don't think/focus on "wrong." Ask, "What's not quite right yet?" This creates a positive mind shift, opens up possibilities.
@LynneaHagen

_____
_____
_____

Section III: How to Get Unstuck

91

Get unstuck. Look at what's not quite right yet, and ask, "What will it take to make it right?". @LynneaHagen

_____

_____

_____

92

Get unstuck. Look at what's "right," and what makes it right, then bring THAT into what you're trying to do. @LynneaHagen

Section III: How to Get Unstuck

93

Get unstuck using role models. Watch what unstuck, high producers do, talk to them, and copy what they do. @LynneaHagen

94

Get unstuck. Embrace your shadow. You strike gold when you turn toward your fear, limiting beliefs and misaligned parts. @tcrausch

95

Release "off-track" thoughts. Write them on slips of paper or in an "ideas journal." File them in a "think about later" spot.
@LynneaHagen

_____

_____

_____

96

Get Unstuck: Hang with people who don't intentionally "push your buttons" & walk away from those who do. @LynneaHagen

97

Get unstuck. Stop insisting how things should look or resisting how they are. To "up" your productivity, focus on the good. @LynneaHagen

98

Get Unstuck: Define your boundaries. List "10 Things That People Can't Do to Me." Do it now, for yourself. @LynneaHagen

---

99

Get unstuck. Make sure others, and YOU, honor and respect your personal boundaries. @LynneaHagen

---

Section III: How to Get Unstuck

100

Get Unstuck: Defend your boundaries. Calmly ask the offender if they realize what they're doing to you. This should stop them. @LynneaHagen

_____
_____
_____

101

Get Unstuck: Defend boundaries. If someone ignores your boundary requests, leave. If they're a subordinate, ask them to leave. @LynneaHagen

102

Get things out of your mind & heart that need to be said. Write the letter. Say "I'm sorry." Tell others what you need. @LynneaHagen

Section III: How to Get Unstuck

103

Get Unstuck. Tell 3 people what you appreciate about them, creating positive energy in your brain & improved relationships. @LynneaHagen

_____
_____
_____

104

Get unstuck. Stop expecting life to be fair. Sometimes it is, sometimes it isn't. Deal with it. Whining only keeps you stuck.
@LynneaHagen

_____
_____
_____

Section III: How to Get Unstuck

105

Get Unstuck: Tell yourself 3 things that you appreciate about you in the mirror. This creates positive energy and self-regard. @LynneaHagen

_____

_____

_____

106

Get unstuck. Fight the battles (YOUR battles only) that are really worth fighting, change what you can, and accept the rest. @LynneaHagen

_____

_____

_____

107

Get unstuck. Plan how you'll handle temptations that could pull you off-track or run counter to your goals. @LynneaHagen

_____

_____

_____

Section III: How to Get Unstuck

108

Get unstuck. Take setbacks in stride. Don't look for scapegoats or lay blame on everyone but yourself. @coachgoldsmith

109

Get unstuck. At some point say, "This is good. This is enough," or you'll never get anything done. Is that what you want? @LynneaHagen

110

Get Unstuck: Don't waste your thoughts and energy trying to change someone else. Work on growing and improving yourself. @LynneaHagen

111

Get Unstuck: Think what's POSSIBLE. It's a mindset, a fuel that connects you to Spirit, Passion, True Desires, Bigger Ideas. @LynneaHagen

112

Fight fear. To learn, grow, and be successful, YOU MUST step out of comfort. All you desire lies on the other side of fear. @bobproctorLIVE

_____
_____
_____

113

Be positively selfish. Take exquisite care of your needs to gain the time, support & energy to do what you're here to do. @LynneaHagen

114

Get unstuck. Think smaller. Break tasks into "chunks," then do a forced prioritization of what to do 1st, 2nd, etc. @LynneaHagen

Section III: How to Get Unstuck

115

Get unstuck: Get a handle on things. For example, do a budget with business and personal expenses. @LynneaHagen

_____

_____

_____

116

Take time to think. Look at all parts of life/business. See what you can identify, eliminate, replace, improve. Then do it.
@LynneaHagen

Section III: How to Get Unstuck

117

Take time to think, without "doing" anything. Think about what you really want, and what's in place now for you to get that. @LynneaHagen

_____
_____
_____

118

Get unstuck. No SHOULDS. Instead, use WOULD, WILL, CAN, COULD, which are less judgmental, opening the mind to possibilities. @LynneaHagen

_____
_____
_____

119

Get unstuck. Take time to think. Define the "4 Ds": doubts, dream-stealers, distractions, disappointments. @LynneaHagen

---

Section III: How to Get Unstuck

120

Get unstuck. Stop multitasking. Research shows it reduces productivity and will make you feel more stuck. Do 1 task at a time. @LynneaHagen

121

Get unstuck. Take time to think. Look at past successes, and what thoughts, actions created those. @LynneaHagen

122

Get unstuck. Ask yourself every hour: Is what I'm doing right now moving me in the direction of my dreams? @LynneaHagen

_____

_____

_____

123

Get unstuck. Take time to think. Decide: What do you want to do next? You truly know the answer, but only if you keep asking. @LynneaHagen

_____

_____

_____

Section III: How to Get Unstuck

124

Get unstuck. Stop putting off little tasks that can be eliminated or outsourced altogether! Find people or systems for these. @LynneaHagen

125

Get unstuck. Say NO to things that aren't essential to your progress, and take the rush out of your life. @LynneaHagen

126

Get unstuck. Know this: You are ONLY stuck if you think you are! Choose to see your situation in a new way. @connectingqueen

Section III: How to Get Unstuck

127

Get unstuck. Release hurry & impatience, and affirm that you have time & energy to do what is yours to do. @LynneaHagen

_____

_____

_____

128

Get unstuck. Decide what things slow you down or pull you off-track. Then stop doing those things. @LynneaHagen

_____

_____

_____

Section III: How to Get Unstuck

129

Get unstuck. Stop giving away your time or knowledge for free or for non-productive results. @LynneaHagen

130

Get unstuck. Celebrate YOU & each little movement forward. Give yourself "high 5s" or back pats for even small accomplishments. @LynneaHagen

131

Get Unstuck. Perfection is the obstacle of creation & achievement. Done outweighs perfect, so get 'er done & tweak it later.
@LynneaHagen

132

Stay unstuck by always challenging yourself to decide that a project is complete. Perfection is rarely productive.
@LynneaHagen

Section IV
Get Going and Stay Unstuck

Once you feel that you are back on track and energized, how will you stay there? It's essential to stay in tune, on track, and aligned with your goals and dreams. In this section are thoughts on how to stay unstuck. If you feel yourself slipping, just go back to chapter 3.

Here are bonus "shareable" tips for staying unstuck:

Stay unstuck. In all you are and do, operate and think to the highest standards and integrity. @LynneaHagen

Always look for good, beautiful things. Your world is shouting out, revealing something glorious to energize and inspire you. @LynneaHagen

Section IV: Get Going and Stay Unstuck

133

Stay Unstuck: Create your own "Board of Directors" for accountability, wisdom, and insight. @LynneaHagen

134

Stay unstuck. If you're a paranoid, be an Inverse Paranoid. Say, "I believe that the Universe is conspiring to HELP me!" @LynneaHagen

135

Stay unstuck. If you adopt the belief, "There is always a way," it will ensure that you will get unstuck every time! @connectingqueen

136

Stay Unstuck: Claim your values for living. Put them into practice. Your values will propel you to authentic great work. @tcrausch

137

Stay Unstuck. Remember, the negative voice is a liar. Notice it, but don't believe it. Learn from it, change it, and move on.
@LynneaHagen

138

List the positives. In good times, create a list of all things going really well in your life. Keep it handy for tough times.
@LynneaHagen

Section IV: Get Going and Stay Unstuck

139

Weeds grow automatically, even in our minds. Every day, stand guard at the door of your mind, and feed it something good. @tonyrobbins

140

Stay unstuck. Continue to surround yourself with people who inspire you, support you, and believe in you (& vice versa).
@LynneaHagen

About the Author

Lynnea Hagen, **MS** is an organizational development consultant, focusing on Higher Ground Leadership™ Development and strategic business plans. She combines strong business experience with tools and techniques to help the client grow as a human being and leader - all coupled with inspiration and humor.

Lynnea holds several coaching certifications, including Executives and Groups, and an MS in Organizational Development from University of San Francisco. In 25+ years of coaching and consulting, including retreats for leaders and their teams, she has helped hundreds of organizations and their people achieve more, with greater satisfaction, in less time. Lynnea is the creator of the Ecosystem of Success (**ecosystemofsuccess.com**). She is also a best-selling author, radio host of "Abundance Leadership," speaker, and trainer. Her company's mission is to create organizations that inspire the soul. This creates a 3-way win: productivity, profits, and people.

What Are Your Ahas?

Thanks for reading *Lynnea Hagen on Stuckness*!

Got any "AhaMessages" that would fit with this book?

We'd love for you to share them!

Tweet us **@happyabout** and/or **@LynneaHagen**, and tag it with **#stuckness**.

Amplifier™
Democratizing Thought Leadership

The Aha Amplifier™ is the only thought leadership platform with a built in marketplace making it easy to share curated content from like-minded thought leaders. There are over 25k diverse AhaMessages™ from thought leaders from around the world.

The Aha Amplifier makes it easy to create, organize and share your own thought leadership AhaMessages in digestible, bite-sized morsels. Users are able to democratize thought leadership in their organizations by: 1) Making it easy for any advocate to share existing content with their Twitter, Facebook, LinkedIn & Google+ networks. 2) Allowing internal experts to create their own thought leadership content, and 3) Encouraging the expert's advocates to share that content on their networks.

The experience of many authors is that they have been able to create their social media enabled AhaBooks™ of 140 AhaMessages in less than a day.

Sign up for a free account at
http://www.AhaAmplifier.com today!

Please pick up a copy of this book in the Aha Amplifier and share each AhaMessage socially at
http://aha.pub/stuckness

www.ingramcontent.com/pod-product-compliance
Ingram Content Group UK Ltd.
Pitfield, Milton Keynes, MK11 3LW, UK
UKHW021303180426
11947UKWH00015B/996